Little Pebble™

Habitats

T0052300

All About Forests

by Christina Mia Gardeski

CAPSTONE PRESS
a capstone imprint

Little Pebble is published by Capstone Press,
1710 Roe Crest Drive, North Mankato, Minnesota 56003
www.mycapstone.com

Copyright © 2018 by Capstone Press, a Capstone imprint. All rights reserved. No part of this publication may be reproduced in whole or in part, or stored in a retrieval system, or transmitted in any form or by any means, electronic, mechanical, photocopying, recording, or otherwise, without written permission of the publisher.

Library of Congress Cataloging-in-Publication Data
Names: Gardeski, Christina Mia, author.
Title: All about forests / by Christina Mia Gardeski.
Description: North Mankato, Minnesota : Capstone Press, [2017] | Series: Little pebble. Habitats | Includes bibliographical references and index.
Identifiers: LCCN 2017004645 (print) | LCCN 2017006585 (ebook) | ISBN 9781515776383 (library binding) | ISBN 9781515776468 (pbk.) | ISBN 9781515776772 (eBook PDF)
Subjects: LCSH: Forest ecology—Juvenile literature. | Forests and forestry—Juvenile literature.
Classification: LCC QH541.5.F6 G368 2017 (print) | LCC QH541.5.F6 (ebook) | DDC 577.3—dc23
LC record available at https://lccn.loc.gov/2017004645

Editorial Credits
Nick Healy, editor; Kayla Dohmen, designer; Wanda Winch, media researcher; Steve Walker, production specialist

Photo Credits
Dreamstime: Bchancha, 21, Betty4240, 15, Lucidwaters, 11; Shutterstock: David Boutin, 7, Erik Mandre, 1, Ermakov Alexander, 17, Grigoriy Pil, 9, Helena-art, tree design, Henrik Larsson, 19, Jeff Feverston, cover, jurra8, 13, Sara van Netten, 5

Printed in the United States 5914

Table of Contents

What Is a Forest? 4

In the Treetops 10

On the Ground 14

Growing Up 20

Glossary 22
Read More 23
Internet Sites 23
Index 24

What Is a Forest?

A forest is a land of trees.

The trees grow close together.

Some trees have leaves.

The leaves change color in fall.

They fall off by winter.

Other trees have needles.

They stay green all year.

In the Treetops

The trees grow tall.

Branches cover the forest.

It is a shady habitat.

Many animals live here.

Owls spy on mice.

Squirrels pick acorns.

owl

On the Ground

Some trees fall.

Skunks live in the old logs.

Snakes hide under logs.

skunks

Mushrooms grow on the logs.

Deer eat the mushrooms.

Ants eat the old wood.

The wood turns into soil.

Growing Up

Animals carry seeds.

Seeds blow in the wind.

Seeds fall in the soil.

The forest grows.

Glossary

acorn—the seed of an oak tree

forest—land filled with trees that grow close together

habitat—the home of a plant or animal

leaf—part of a plant that grows from the stem

log—a big tree trunk that has been cut down or has fallen to the ground

mushroom—a fungus with a stem and flat cap

needle—the leaf of an evergreen tree

soil—dirt in which plants can grow

treetop—the top of a tree